I0421410

MASTERING AMAZON FBA
(2024 & BEYOND)

Unlock the Secrets of Selling on Amazon, Boost Your
Business, and Thrive in the Competitive Marketplace

TRACI FISCHER

Welcome to Your Amazon FBA Journey!

In this comprehensive guide, discover the strategies and insights that will transform your Amazon FBA business. Whether you're a novice or an experienced seller, this book equips you with the tools needed to excel in the world's largest online marketplace.

What's Inside?

I. Uncover the Foundations

A. Overview of Amazon FBA: Understand the powerhouse that is Amazon FBA.

B. Benefits of Selling on Amazon: Explore the advantages that set Amazon FBA apart.

C. Key Terms and Concepts: Navigate the Amazon ecosystem with confidence.

II. Launch Your Amazon FBA Adventure

A. Account Setup: Seamlessly establish your Amazon FBA account.

B. Product Selection: Uncover the art and science of selecting winning products.

C. Understanding Amazon's Policies: Navigate the policies crucial for your success.

III. Set Up Your Amazon FBA Business

A. Creating Product Listings: Craft compelling listings that captivate your audience.

B. Pricing Strategies: Master the art of pricing for profitability.

C. Managing Inventory: Explore effective inventory management techniques.

IV. Fulfillment and Shipping

A. How Amazon FBA Works: Unravel the mechanics behind seamless fulfillment.

B. Shipping and Labeling Requirements: Stay compliant and optimize your shipping processes.

C. Handling Returns and Customer Service: Delve into strategies for exceptional customer service.

V. Optimize Your Amazon FBA Business

A. Marketing Strategies:Propel your products into the limelight.

B. Monitoring and Analyzing Performance: Leverage data for informed decision-making.

C. Scaling Your Business: Uncover the secrets to sustainable growth.

VI. Challenges and Solutions

A. Common Pitfalls: Learn from common pitfalls to avoid potential setbacks.

B. Overcoming Challenges: Strategize your way through obstacles with confidence.

C. Staying Competitive in the Marketplace: Adopt winning strategies to stay ahead.

VII. Advanced Strategies

A. Expanding Product Lines:Diversify your offerings strategically.

B. International Selling: Unlock the global potential of Amazon FBA.

C. Leveraging Amazon FBA Tools: Harness the power of cutting-edge tools for success.

VIII. Financial Management in Amazon FBA

A. Budgeting and Cost Analysis: Optimize your financial strategies.

B. Profit Margins and Pricing Strategies: Maximize profitability with strategic pricing.

C. Managing Cash Flow: Navigate the financial currents with confidence.

IX. Building a Brand Presence on Amazon

A. Branding Strategies for FBA Sellers: Create a compelling brand identity.

B. Establishing Brand Authority: Cultivate trust and credibility in the marketplace.

C. Leveraging Brand Registry: Secure your brand's rightful place on Amazon.

X. Customer Engagement and Loyalty

A. Creating Exceptional Customer Experiences: Elevate your customer service game.

B. Implementing Customer Loyalty Programs: Foster lasting connections with your customers.

C. Utilizing Customer Feedback for Improvement: Turn feedback into a tool for growth.

XI. Additional Insights for Success

A. Financial Management: Dive deep into budgeting, profit margins, and cash flow.

B. Building Partnerships and Collaborations: Forge alliances for mutual growth.

C. Continuous Learning and Adaptation: Stay ahead with evolving e-commerce trends.

Don't miss out on the strategies, tips, and insights that will propel your Amazon FBA business to new heights. Turn the pages and embark on a journey to e-commerce mastery!

CONTENTS

INTRODUCTION

Amazon Fulfillment by Amazon (FBA) is a comprehensive service offered by the e-commerce giant, revolutionizing the landscape of online retail. At its core, Amazon FBA allows sellers to outsource the logistical aspects of their business, enabling them to store products in Amazon's fulfillment centers. This strategic approach shifts responsibilities such as packing, shipping, and customer service to Amazon, providing sellers with a streamlined and efficient way to conduct their business.

The backbone of Amazon FBA is the vast network of fulfillment centers strategically located around the world. These centers are equipped with cutting-edge technology to handle inventory, manage orders, and ensure timely deliveries. This infrastructure enables sellers to leverage Amazon's extensive resources, providing a competitive edge in the highly dynamic e-commerce market.

Benefits of Selling on Amazon FBA

1. Prime Membership Advantage: Products fulfilled by Amazon are often eligible for Amazon Prime, a subscription service with

millions of members. Sellers on FBA benefit from increased visibility and the potential to attract a broader customer base.

2. Effortless Logistics: One of the primary advantages of FBA is the seamless handling of logistics. Sellers no longer need to worry about packing, shipping, and managing inventory, allowing them to focus on scaling their business and enhancing the quality of their products.

3. Customer Trust and Satisfaction: Amazon's reputation for reliability and customer satisfaction extends to products fulfilled by Amazon. With the FBA label, customers are

more likely to trust the shipping and delivery process, leading to positive reviews and repeat business.

4. Global Reach: Amazon FBA opens doors to international markets, enabling sellers to reach customers worldwide. The global distribution network ensures prompt and efficient deliveries, making it easier for sellers to expand their reach beyond domestic borders.

Key Terms and Concepts

1. Fulfillment Centers: These are strategically located warehouses where sellers' products

are stored, processed, and shipped. Amazon's fulfillment centers play a pivotal role in the smooth operation of FBA.

2. Inventory Management: Efficient management of stock is crucial for FBA success. This involves monitoring stock levels, restocking inventory, and ensuring that products are readily available for customers.

3. Order Fulfillment: The process of receiving, processing, and delivering customer orders. With FBA, Amazon takes charge of order fulfillment, offering a hassle-free experience for both sellers and customers.

4. Storage Fees: Sellers using FBA are subject to storage fees based on the space their products occupy in Amazon's fulfillment centers. Understanding and managing these fees is essential for cost-effective inventory management.

5. FBA Labeling and Packaging Requirements: Amazon has specific guidelines for labeling and packaging products enrolled in the FBA program. Adhering to these requirements is crucial to ensure smooth processing within the fulfillment centers.

Delving into the world of Amazon FBA offers sellers a powerful platform to streamline operations, enhance customer experiences, and tap into a global market. Understanding the benefits and key terms associated with FBA lays the foundation for a successful and sustainable e-commerce venture on the Amazon platform.

GETTING STARTED WITH AMAZON FBA

Account Setup

Establishing an Amazon FBA business begins with the crucial step of account setup. Navigate to the Amazon Seller Central platform to create an account, choosing between an individual or professional seller account. The individual account suits those with limited sales volume, while the professional account is designed for high-volume sellers. Complete the necessary registration steps, providing accurate business information, tax details, and payment preferences.

Once the account is active, sellers gain access to the FBA dashboard within Seller Central. This dashboard serves as the control center for managing inventory, monitoring sales, and accessing various tools provided by Amazon to streamline the selling process.

Product Selection

The success of an Amazon FBA venture heavily relies on strategic product selection. Sellers should conduct thorough market research to identify profitable niches and trending products. Consider factors such as demand, competition, and profit margins when evaluating potential items to sell.

Additionally, leverage Amazon's product ranking and review system to gauge customer interest and satisfaction. Products with high demand and positive reviews often fare well on the platform. Utilize tools like the Amazon Best Sellers list and product research software to refine your product selection strategy.

Diversifying your product portfolio and identifying unique offerings can set your FBA business apart from competitors. Ensure that chosen products align with your business goals and fit within the guidelines of Amazon's policies.

Understanding Amazon's Policies

Navigating Amazon's policies is essential for FBA sellers to maintain a healthy and compliant business. Familiarize yourself with Amazon's Seller Policies and Seller Code of Conduct, which outline the rules and regulations governing seller behavior on the platform.

Key policy areas include product listings, customer communication, pricing, and fulfillment requirements. Pay close attention to prohibited items and restricted categories to avoid potential pitfalls. Staying informed about policy updates is crucial, as Amazon may revise its guidelines to adapt to industry changes and customer expectations.

Fulfillment policies, including packaging and labeling requirements, are integral to successful FBA operations. Adhering to these guidelines ensures that products move smoothly through Amazon's fulfillment centers, reducing the risk of delays or issues with order processing.

Regularly monitor communication channels from Amazon, such as Seller Central notifications and policy update emails, to stay abreast of any changes. This proactive approach not only ensures compliance but also positions your FBA business for sustained growth within the Amazon marketplace.

Getting started with Amazon FBA involves setting up your seller account, conducting strategic product research, and understanding and adhering to Amazon's policies. A solid foundation in these areas establishes a platform for success, allowing you to focus on growing your business and providing a positive experience for your customers.

SETTING UP YOUR AMAZON FBA BUSINESS

Creating Product Listings

Crafting compelling product listings is a fundamental aspect of establishing a successful Amazon FBA business. Begin by conducting thorough keyword research to optimize product titles, bullet points, and descriptions for search visibility. Use relevant and high-traffic keywords to enhance your product's discoverability in Amazon's vast marketplace.

Accompany your product listings with high-quality images showcasing the item from various angles. Amazon allows multiple images, and presenting your product in a visually appealing manner can significantly impact buyer confidence. Additionally, include detailed and accurate product information, specifications, and features to assist customers in making informed purchasing decisions.

Leverage Enhanced Brand Content or A+ Content (for eligible sellers) to further enhance your product listings. This feature enables you to include additional visuals, detailed product descriptions, and brand storytelling, creating a more engaging and informative shopping experience.

Pricing Strategies

Implementing effective pricing strategies is crucial for maximizing profits and staying competitive on Amazon. Begin by researching competitors' pricing and evaluating the perceived value of your product within the market. Consider factors such as product quality, brand reputation, and unique selling points when determining your pricing strategy.

Utilize Amazon's automated pricing tools or third-party pricing software to dynamically adjust your prices based on market fluctuations, demand, and competitor pricing changes. This approach ensures that your prices remain competitive and reflective of current market conditions.

Factor in all costs associated with your FBA business, including Amazon fees, fulfillment fees, and shipping costs, to establish a profitable yet competitive price point. Striking the right balance between affordability and profitability is key to attracting customers and maximizing sales.

Managing Inventory

Efficient inventory management is vital for preventing stockouts, minimizing storage costs, and optimizing overall FBA operations. Leverage Amazon's inventory management tools to monitor stock levels, set reorder thresholds, and receive alerts for low inventory.

Implement the "Just-in-Time" (JIT) inventory strategy to minimize storage fees and ensure a steady flow of products to meet customer demand. Regularly assess the sales velocity of each product and adjust your inventory levels accordingly. Consider seasonal trends, promotions, and upcoming events when planning your inventory.

Stay proactive in managing slow-moving or stagnant inventory. Implementing promotional strategies, such as discounts or bundling, can help move inventory and prevent storage fees from accumulating. Additionally, periodically assess and update your product catalog to align with market trends and consumer preferences.

Utilize Amazon's FBA Restock Inventory tool to receive recommendations on when and how much to replenish. This tool considers factors like sales history, current inventory levels, and upcoming demand, providing valuable insights to streamline your restocking process.

Setting up your Amazon FBA business involves creating compelling product listings, implementing effective pricing strategies, and adopting efficient inventory management practices. A well-optimized and strategically priced product, combined with streamlined inventory operations, positions your FBA business for sustained growth and success on the Amazon platform.

FULFILLMENT AND SHIPPING

How Amazon FBA Works

Understanding how Amazon FBA works is pivotal for sellers looking to leverage the platform's extensive fulfillment network. Upon enrolling products in the FBA program, sellers send their inventory to Amazon's fulfillment centers. Amazon takes on the responsibility of storing, picking, packing, and shipping products to customers when orders are placed.

The process begins with sellers preparing their products according to Amazon's packaging and labeling requirements. Once received at the fulfillment center, the inventory is scanned, sorted, and stored. When a customer places an order, Amazon automatically picks the product, packages it, and ships it to the customer on behalf of the seller.

Amazon FBA also provides sellers with the advantage of Prime eligibility, allowing their products to be offered with the coveted Amazon Prime badge. Prime-eligible products benefit from faster shipping times, enhancing customer satisfaction and potentially increasing sales.

Shipping and Labeling Requirements

Complying with Amazon's shipping and labeling requirements is crucial for seamless processing within the fulfillment centers. Ensure that products are packaged securely and labeled following Amazon's guidelines. Each unit must have a scannable barcode, typically an FNSKU or UPC, affixed to facilitate accurate tracking and fulfillment.

Utilize Amazon's shipping tools to create shipping plans and generate shipping labels. Clearly communicate with carriers to ensure timely and accurate delivery of inventory to the designated fulfillment centers. Amazon may provide discounted shipping rates through their partnered carriers, offering cost-effective solutions for sellers.

Stay informed about any updates to shipping and labeling policies to avoid potential disruptions to your FBA operations. Accurate and compliant packaging not only expedites the fulfillment process but also contributes to a positive customer experience.

Handling Returns and Customer Service

Amazon FBA simplifies the process of handling returns and customer service, alleviating much of the burden from sellers. When a customer initiates a return, Amazon manages the return process, including product inspections and restocking. This streamlined approach ensures a consistent and customer-friendly return experience.

Sellers should regularly monitor and address customer inquiries through the Amazon Seller Central platform. Timely and helpful responses contribute to positive reviews and customer satisfaction. Utilize Amazon's messaging system to communicate with customers and resolve any issues promptly.

In cases where customers encounter problems with FBA orders, Amazon's customer service team takes the lead in resolving issues. Sellers should be aware of Amazon's customer service policies and collaborate with the platform to ensure a high standard of service.

Continuously monitor customer feedback and reviews to identify areas for improvement. Proactive customer service not only fosters positive buyer-seller relationships but also contributes to a strong seller reputation within the Amazon marketplace.

Navigating the fulfillment and shipping aspects of Amazon FBA involves understanding the workflow, adhering to shipping and labeling requirements, and effectively managing returns and customer service. Leveraging the resources and support provided by Amazon FBA enhances the overall efficiency and customer experience, contributing to the long-term success of your e-commerce venture.

OPTIMIZING YOUR AMAZON FBA BUSINESS

Marketing Strategies

Crafting effective marketing strategies is essential for optimizing your Amazon FBA business and boosting product visibility. Utilize Amazon's advertising platform, including Sponsored Products and Sponsored Brands, to strategically promote your products. Leverage relevant keywords, compelling ad copy, and eye-catching visuals to capture the attention of potential customers.

Implementing Amazon's Enhanced Brand Content or A+ Content (for brand registered sellers) allows you to enhance product listings with engaging visuals, detailed descriptions, and brand storytelling. This not only contributes to a more immersive shopping experience but also establishes brand identity and credibility.

Leverage external marketing channels, such as social media and email marketing, to drive traffic to your Amazon listings. Create cohesive cross-channel campaigns to increase brand awareness and attract a broader audience to your FBA products.

Monitoring and Analyzing Performance

Regularly monitoring and analyzing the performance of your Amazon FBA business is crucial for making informed decisions and optimizing your operations. Utilize the analytics tools provided by Amazon Seller Central to track key performance metrics, including sales, conversion rates, and customer feedback.

- Dive into detailed reports to identify top-performing products, analyze customer behavior, and gain insights into market trends. Leverage this data to refine your product selection, adjust pricing strategies, and enhance your overall business strategy.

- Pay close attention to customer reviews and ratings. Positive reviews contribute to a strong seller reputation, while negative feedback offers valuable insights for improvement. Responding to customer reviews, both positive and negative, demonstrates a commitment to customer satisfaction.

Scaling Your Business

Scaling your Amazon FBA business involves strategically expanding your product offerings, entering new markets, and optimizing operational efficiency. Diversify your product catalog based on market demand and trends, continually exploring new opportunities for growth.

- Explore international marketplaces to reach a global audience. Utilize Amazon's tools and resources for international selling, adapting your marketing and pricing strategies to cater to diverse customer preferences.

- Implement efficient inventory management practices to accommodate increased demand. Leverage Amazon's FBA tools to forecast demand, optimize stock levels, and minimize storage costs. Consider investing in automation and technology solutions to streamline order processing and fulfillment.

- Explore partnerships and collaborations within the Amazon ecosystem. Joining the Amazon Brand Registry, for instance, offers additional tools for brand protection and marketing. Collaborate with influencers or participate in Amazon's affiliate program to expand your reach and attract new customers.

Continuously evaluate and adapt your business strategy as market dynamics evolve. Stay informed about industry trends, competitor activities, and changes in consumer behavior. Flexibility and agility are key when scaling your Amazon FBA business for sustained success.

Optimizing your Amazon FBA business involves implementing effective marketing strategies, closely monitoring performance metrics, and strategically scaling your operations. Embracing innovation, staying attuned to market dynamics, and leveraging the resources provided by Amazon FBA position your business for growth and long-term success on the e-commerce platform.

CHALLENGES AND SOLUTIONS

Common Pitfalls

1. Inventory Mismanagement:Inadequate control over inventory levels can lead to stockouts or overstock situations. Sellers must regularly assess demand, monitor sales velocity, and adjust inventory levels accordingly to avoid these pitfalls.

2. Inaccurate Product Listings: Providing incomplete or inaccurate information in product listings can result in dissatisfied customers and negative reviews. Ensure that

listings are detailed, accurate, and comply with Amazon's guidelines to maintain customer trust.

3. Ignoring Customer Feedback: Neglecting customer reviews and feedback can be detrimental. Sellers should actively engage with customers, address concerns, and use feedback to make improvements, fostering a positive seller reputation.

4.Overlooking Amazon Policies: Violating Amazon's policies, whether intentional or unintentional, can lead to account suspension or other penalties. Staying informed about and adhering to Amazon's guidelines is crucial for a successful FBA business.

Overcoming Challenges

1. Implement Robust Inventory Management: Utilize Amazon's FBA tools to monitor inventory levels, set reorder thresholds, and forecast demand. Regularly assess sales trends and adjust inventory accordingly to prevent stockouts or excessive storage fees.

2. Optimize Product Listings: Regularly update and enhance product listings with accurate information, high-quality images, and compelling descriptions. Utilize tools like

A+ Content to create more engaging product pages, improving the overall shopping experience.

3. Proactive Customer Engagement: Actively monitor customer feedback and reviews, responding promptly to address concerns and resolve issues. Establishing strong communication channels with customers can help build trust and loyalty.

4. Continuous Compliance Monitoring: Stay vigilant about changes in Amazon's policies and guidelines. Regularly review the Seller Policies and Seller Code of Conduct to ensure

ongoing compliance, preventing potential issues that could impact your business.

Staying Competitive in the Marketplace

1. Strategic Pricing: Regularly analyze market trends and adjust pricing strategies to remain competitive. Utilize dynamic pricing tools to adapt to changes in demand, competitor pricing, and market conditions.

2. Invest in Marketing: Implement effective marketing strategies, both on and off the Amazon platform. Leverage Amazon's advertising tools, explore external marketing

channels, and invest in brand-building initiatives to enhance visibility and attract customers.

3.Optimize Fulfillment: Offer competitive shipping options and leverage the benefits of Amazon FBA, such as Prime eligibility. Efficient order fulfillment and timely shipping contribute to a positive customer experience, enhancing your competitiveness in the marketplace.

4. Differentiate Your Brand: Stand out by emphasizing unique selling points, building a strong brand identity, and providing exceptional customer service. Consider

product bundling, exclusive offerings, or innovative packaging to set your products apart.

Overcoming challenges and staying competitive in the Amazon FBA marketplace requires a proactive and strategic approach. By addressing common pitfalls, implementing effective solutions, and continuously adapting to market dynamics, sellers can position themselves for long-term success in the ever-evolving e-commerce landscape.

Expanding Product Lines

1. Market Research: Conduct in-depth market research to identify gaps in the market and emerging trends. Analyze customer preferences, competitor offerings, and potential niches to inform your product expansion strategy.

2. Diversification: Consider diversifying your product catalog by introducing complementary or related items. This not only broadens your customer base but also

creates opportunities for cross-selling and upselling.

3. Private Labeling: Explore the option of private labeling to create unique and exclusive products. Building a strong brand around private-label items can contribute to customer loyalty and differentiation in a competitive marketplace.

4. Seasonal Offerings: Introduce seasonal products to capitalize on trends and peak buying seasons. This strategic approach allows your FBA business to remain dynamic and responsive to changing consumer demands throughout the year.

International Selling

1.Research Target Markets: Before expanding internationally, thoroughly research and identify target markets. Consider factors such as cultural differences, regulatory requirements, and local competition to tailor your approach to each market.

2. Optimize Listings for Local Markets: Adapt product listings to cater to the preferences and language of the target market. Utilize translation services if necessary and consider localizing marketing strategies to resonate with the cultural nuances of each region.

3. Understand Cross-Border Logistics: Familiarize yourself with cross-border logistics to ensure smooth shipping and customs clearance. Leverage Amazon's Global Export and Import services to simplify international shipping processes.

4. Currency Considerations: Be mindful of currency exchange rates and pricing strategies when selling internationally. Pricing products in local currencies and offering competitive exchange rates can enhance your appeal to international customers.

Leveraging Amazon FBA Tools

1. Inventory Placement Services: Optimize shipping costs and delivery times by utilizing Amazon's Inventory Placement Services. This feature allows you to send inventory to a single fulfillment center, streamlining the distribution process.

2. FBA Export Program: Expand your customer reach by enrolling in the FBA Export Program. This initiative allows your products to be shipped to international customers even if you're not actively selling in that particular marketplace.

3. Fulfillment Reports: Regularly analyze Fulfillment Reports provided by Amazon to gain insights into your inventory performance, order defects, and customer returns. Use this data to refine your inventory management and customer service strategies.

4. Promotions and Deals: Utilize Amazon's promotional tools to run deals, discounts, or limited-time offers. This can boost product visibility, attract new customers, and stimulate sales. Experiment with various promotional strategies to find what resonates best with your target audience.

Advanced strategies in Amazon FBA involve expanding product lines to meet market demands, venturing into international selling with careful planning, and leveraging the array of tools provided by Amazon FBA to optimize operations. These approaches contribute to the evolution and sustained growth of your e-commerce business within the competitive landscape of Amazon.

FINANCIAL MANAGEMENT IN AMAZON FBA

Budgeting and Cost Analysis

1. Start-up Costs: Begin by meticulously estimating the initial costs of launching your Amazon FBA business. This includes product sourcing, shipping, Amazon seller fees, and any other associated expenses. A detailed budget helps you set realistic financial expectations and plan accordingly.

2. Operational Expenses: Outline ongoing operational costs such as storage fees, fulfillment fees, advertising expenses, and

potential software subscriptions. Regularly review and adjust these budgets as your business evolves to maintain a clear understanding of your financial commitments.

3. Advertising Budget: Allocate a specific budget for advertising within Amazon, taking advantage of tools like Sponsored Products and Sponsored Brands. Regularly evaluate the performance of your advertising campaigns and adjust the budget based on the return on investment (ROI).

4.Contingency Fund: Include a contingency fund in your budget to account for unforeseen expenses or fluctuations in demand. A well-prepared budget with contingency ensures you are better equipped to navigate unexpected financial challenges.

Profit Margins and Pricing Strategies

1. Cost Calculation: Accurately calculate the total cost of each product, including manufacturing, shipping, Amazon fees, and any additional expenses. Understanding your true costs is essential for setting competitive yet profitable prices.

2. Competitor Analysis: Regularly analyze competitor pricing within your niche. This

helps you position your products competitively while maintaining healthy profit margins. Consider factors like perceived value, quality, and unique selling points when determining your pricing strategy.

3. Dynamic Pricing: Utilize dynamic pricing strategies to adjust prices based on market conditions, competitor pricing, and demand fluctuations. Automated pricing tools can assist in real-time adjustments, helping you stay competitive while optimizing profitability.

4. Bundle and Upsell: Explore bundling complementary products or offering upsells

to maximize the value of each transaction. This can contribute to increased average order value and enhanced overall profitability.

Managing Cash Flow

1.Inventory Turnover: Efficiently manage inventory turnover to maintain a healthy cash flow. Avoid overstock situations that tie up capital and lead to increased storage fees. Conversely, minimize stockouts by aligning inventory levels with demand.

2. Payment Terms Negotiation: When working with suppliers, negotiate favorable payment terms to align with your cash flow cycle.

Extending payment terms or securing discounts for early payments can positively impact your overall financial health.

3. Reinvestment Strategies: Develop a strategy for reinvesting profits into inventory, marketing, and other areas that contribute to business growth. Balancing cash flow with strategic reinvestment ensures a sustainable and scalable business model.

4. Monitor Receivables and Payables: Regularly monitor accounts receivable and accounts payable. Promptly collect payments from customers while optimizing payment

schedules with suppliers. This balance helps maintain a steady cash flow.

Effective financial management in Amazon FBA involves meticulous budgeting, strategic pricing, and proactive cash flow management. By maintaining a clear understanding of your financial landscape and implementing sound financial practices, you position your FBA business for long-term stability and success in the competitive e-commerce environment.

BUILDING A BRAND PRESENCE ON AMAZON

Branding Strategies for FBA Sellers

1. Brand Identity Development:Start by defining a clear brand identity that resonates with your target audience. This includes crafting a compelling brand story, establishing a unique value proposition, and creating a memorable brand name and logo. Consistency in visual elements and messaging across your product listings contributes to brand recognition.

2. Branded Packaging: Leverage packaging as a branding tool. Consider investing in branded packaging that not only protects your products but also enhances the unboxing experience for customers. Branded packaging reinforces your brand identity and can contribute to positive customer perceptions.

3. Unique Selling Proposition (USP): Clearly articulate your Unique Selling Proposition—what sets your products apart from the competition. Highlighting distinctive features, superior quality, or additional benefits helps create a strong brand image in the minds of consumers.

4. Brand Voice and Messaging: Develop a consistent brand voice in your product listings, marketing materials, and customer communications. Align your messaging with your target audience's preferences and values, fostering a connection that goes beyond the transactional nature of e-commerce.

Establishing Brand Authority

1. Content Marketing: Create informative and valuable content related to your products or industry. This can take the form of blog posts, how-to guides, or educational videos. Establishing your brand as an authority in

your niche builds trust with customers and enhances your credibility.

2. Customer Reviews and Testimonials: Encourage satisfied customers to leave positive reviews and testimonials. Authentic feedback serves as social proof and can influence potential buyers. Address any negative reviews promptly and professionally to demonstrate your commitment to customer satisfaction.

3.Partnerships and Collaborations: Explore partnerships with influencers, industry experts, or other reputable brands. Collaborative efforts can amplify your brand's reach and reinforce its authority within the Amazon marketplace.

4. Thought Leadership: Position yourself as a thought leader in your niche by sharing insights, trends, and expertise. This can be achieved through participating in relevant forums, contributing to industry publications, or hosting webinars. Thought leadership enhances brand authority and visibility.

Leveraging Brand Registry

1. Benefits of Brand Registry: Enroll in Amazon Brand Registry to access exclusive tools and benefits. Brand Registry helps

protect your intellectual property, offering features like brand-specific search algorithms, enhanced content creation, and proactive measures against counterfeiters. 2. Trademark Registration: To enroll in Brand Registry, you generally need a registered trademark for your brand. Consider trademarking your brand name and logo to secure your intellectual property rights and strengthen your position on the Amazon platform.

3. Enhanced Brand Content (EBC): Brand Registry enables access to Enhanced Brand Content (EBC), allowing you to create visually

appealing and informative product listings. EBC enhances the shopping experience for customers and contributes to increased conversion rates.

4. Brand Analytics: Utilize Brand Analytics, a tool available through Brand Registry, to gain insights into customer behavior, market trends, and competitor data. These insights inform strategic decisions, allowing you to optimize your brand presence on Amazon.

In summary, building a brand presence on Amazon involves strategic branding, establishing authority, and leveraging the benefits of Brand Registry. By creating a compelling brand identity, demonstrating expertise, and protecting your intellectual property, you can foster customer loyalty and position your FBA business for long-term success on the e-commerce platform.

CUSTOMER ENGAGEMENT AND LOYALTY

Creating Exceptional Customer Experiences

1.Responsive Customer Service: Prioritize timely and helpful responses to customer inquiries and issues. Establish clear communication channels through the Amazon Seller Central platform to address queries, provide assistance, and resolve concerns promptly. A responsive approach builds trust and enhances the overall customer experience.

2. Transparent Policies: Clearly communicate your return, refund, and shipping policies to set customer expectations. Transparency fosters trust and minimizes misunderstandings, contributing to positive experiences. Consider incorporating easy-to-understand FAQs within your product listings.

3. Personalization: Tailor your interactions to create a personalized shopping experience. Use customer data to offer personalized recommendations, exclusive discounts, or relevant product bundles. Personalization

enhances the perceived value of your brand and strengthens customer relationships.

4. Post-Purchase Engagement: Engage with customers even after they make a purchase. Follow up with order confirmations, shipping notifications, and post-purchase emails expressing gratitude. Encourage customers to share their experiences and provide feedback, fostering a sense of connection with your brand.

Implementing Customer Loyalty Programs

1. Rewards and Incentives: Develop a customer loyalty program that offers rewards and incentives for repeat purchases. Consider strategies such as tiered discounts, exclusive access to new products, or a points-based system that customers can redeem for future discounts or free items.

2. Early Access and Exclusive Offers: Provide loyal customers with early access to new product launches or exclusive promotions. This not only rewards their loyalty but also

creates a sense of exclusivity, encouraging continued engagement with your brand.

3. Referral Programs: Implement referral programs that incentivize existing customers to refer friends and family. Offer discounts or exclusive perks for both the referrer and the new customer. Word-of-mouth recommendations from satisfied customers can significantly contribute to brand growth.

4. Loyalty Tiers: Introduce loyalty tiers based on customer spending or engagement levels. Higher tiers can offer additional benefits such as faster shipping, dedicated customer support, or exclusive members-only events.

This approach encourages customers to strive for higher loyalty status.

Utilizing Customer Feedback for Improvement

1. Feedback Solicitation: Actively seek customer feedback through post-purchase emails, surveys, and review requests. Make the process simple and encourage customers to share their thoughts on their shopping experience. This valuable input provides insights into strengths and areas for improvement.

2. Analyzing Reviews: Regularly analyze customer reviews to identify common themes, both positive and negative. Positive reviews highlight strengths to leverage, while negative reviews offer opportunities for improvement. Use this feedback loop to refine product quality, packaging, and customer service.

3. Product Iteration: Demonstrate a commitment to continuous improvement by iterating on your products based on customer feedback. If customers consistently request new features or improvements, consider incorporating these suggestions in future

product releases. This proactive approach enhances customer satisfaction.

4. Communication of Changes: When implementing changes based on customer feedback, transparently communicate these updates to your customer base. Acknowledge their input, explain the improvements made, and express gratitude for their contributions. This transparency builds trust and showcases a customer-centric approach.

Customer engagement and loyalty in Amazon FBA involve creating exceptional experiences, implementing effective loyalty programs, and leveraging customer feedback for continuous improvement. By prioritizing customer satisfaction and building lasting relationships, you not only enhance your brand's reputation but also cultivate a loyal customer base that contributes to the sustained success of your FBA business.

LEGAL AND COMPLIANCE CONSIDERATIONS

Intellectual Property Protection

1. Trademark Registration: Prioritize the registration of trademarks for your brand name and logo. Trademarks provide legal protection against unauthorized use, counterfeit products, and brand infringement. Registering your trademarks enhances your ability to enforce intellectual property rights on the Amazon platform.

2. Patents and Design Rights: Depending on your product's nature, consider obtaining

patents or design rights to protect unique features or designs. This legal protection adds a layer of defense against competitors attempting to replicate or imitate your products.

3. Copyright Protection: If applicable, explore copyright protection for creative elements such as product descriptions, images, and marketing materials. Copyright safeguards your original content from unauthorized use, reinforcing your brand's uniqueness.

4. Monitoring and Enforcement: Regularly monitor the marketplace for potential intellectual property infringements. Utilize

Amazon's Brand Registry and other monitoring tools to identify unauthorized sellers and counterfeit products. Swiftly enforce your intellectual property rights through cease and desist letters or, if necessary, legal action.

Taxation and Compliance

1. Tax Identification Number (TIN): Ensure compliance with tax regulations by obtaining a Tax Identification Number (TIN) or Employer Identification Number (EIN) if required. This identification number is essential for tax reporting purposes and

ensures accurate identification of your business entity.

2. Sales Tax Obligations: Understand and comply with sales tax obligations based on your business's location and the jurisdictions in which you sell. Amazon provides tools and services to assist with sales tax collection and remittance, but sellers should stay informed about evolving tax laws and regulations.

3. Income Tax Reporting: Keep detailed financial records and report income accurately for tax purposes. Utilize accounting software or professional services to ensure compliance with income tax regulations.

Consistent and accurate reporting minimizes the risk of audits and penalties.

4. International Tax Considerations: If engaged in international selling, be aware of tax obligations in the countries where you operate. Consider consulting with tax professionals familiar with international taxation to navigate the complexities and ensure compliance with local tax laws.

Understanding Amazon's Terms of Service

1. Seller Code of Conduct: Familiarize yourself with Amazon's Seller Code of Conduct, which outlines the ethical and legal standards

expected of sellers. Adhering to this code is essential for maintaining a positive seller reputation and avoiding account suspensions or penalties.

2. Product Listing Policies: Comply with Amazon's policies related to product listings, including accurate and transparent product information, prohibited content, and restricted categories. Failure to adhere to these guidelines can result in listing removals or account suspensions.

3. Review Policies: Understand Amazon's policies regarding customer reviews, including guidelines on incentivized reviews

and prohibited review practices. Encourage authentic reviews from satisfied customers while avoiding any activities that violate Amazon's review policies.

4. Intellectual Property Policies: Be well-versed in Amazon's policies regarding intellectual property, including the process for reporting and resolving infringement claims. Familiarity with these policies is crucial for both protecting your intellectual property and responding to claims made against your listings.

In summary, legal and compliance considerations in Amazon FBA encompass intellectual property protection, tax obligations, and strict adherence to Amazon's terms of service. Prioritizing these aspects not only ensures legal compliance but also establishes a foundation for long-term success and a positive reputation within the Amazon marketplace.

OPTIMIZING PRODUCT VISIBILITY

Search Engine Optimization (SEO) for Amazon

1. Keyword Research: Conduct thorough keyword research to identify relevant and high-volume search terms for your products. Utilize tools like Amazon's Keyword Tool or third-party options to discover keywords that potential customers are likely to use when searching for products similar to yours.

2. Optimized Product Titles: Craft compelling and informative product titles that incorporate your primary keywords. Ensure

titles are concise, clearly describe the product, and highlight key features. Follow Amazon's guidelines for title length and avoid keyword stuffing.

3. Strategic Product Descriptions: Write detailed and engaging product descriptions that not only appeal to customers but also incorporate relevant keywords naturally. Focus on providing valuable information about the product's benefits, features, and use cases.

4. Utilizing Backend Keywords: Take advantage of backend keywords in Seller Central to include additional relevant terms

that may not fit organically in your product listing. These keywords help improve the discoverability of your products within Amazon's search algorithm.

Using Amazon PPC Advertising Effectively

1. Keyword Targeting: Develop targeted and relevant keyword lists for your PPC campaigns. Utilize both broad and exact match types to capture a wide range of search queries while maintaining control over ad relevance.

2. Compelling Ad Copy: Craft compelling ad copy that highlights unique selling points, promotions, or discounts. Emphasize what sets your products apart and entices customers to click on your ad.

3. Optimized Product Images: Ensure your product images are visually appealing and provide a clear representation of your products. High-quality images not only attract attention but also contribute to a positive user experience, potentially leading to higher click-through rates.

4. Regular Campaign Monitoring: Continuously monitor the performance of

your PPC campaigns. Analyze metrics such as click-through rate (CTR), conversion rate, and cost per click (CPC). Use this data to optimize your campaigns, adjusting bids and refining keyword targeting for better results.

Winning the Buy Box Strategies

1. Competitive Pricing: Price your products competitively to increase the likelihood of winning the Buy Box. Consider factors such as fulfillment method, shipping costs, and overall value when determining your pricing strategy.

2. Maintaining High Performance Metrics: Focus on maintaining high seller performance

metrics, including order defect rate, late shipment rate, and positive feedback. Amazon prioritizes sellers with excellent performance, increasing the chances of winning the Buy Box.

3. Utilizing FBA: If feasible, leverage Fulfillment by Amazon (FBA) to fulfill your orders. FBA offers fast and reliable shipping, contributing to a positive customer experience and enhancing your eligibility for the Buy Box.

4. Inventory Management: Ensure sufficient inventory levels to prevent stockouts, as running out of stock negatively impacts your

chances of winning the Buy Box. Utilize tools like Amazon's Restock Inventory feature to optimize your inventory management.

Optimizing product visibility on Amazon involves strategic use of SEO, effective Amazon PPC advertising, and employing winning strategies to secure the Buy Box. By implementing these techniques, sellers can enhance the discoverability of their products, attract more customers, and ultimately drive sales within the competitive Amazon marketplace.

ADVANCED ANALYTICS AND DATA-DRIVEN DECISIONS

Harnessing Big Data in FBA

1. Data Sources and Collection: Identify and aggregate data from various sources within your Amazon FBA business, including sales data, customer behavior, advertising metrics, and inventory levels. Utilize Amazon's Seller Central analytics tools and consider third-party analytics solutions for comprehensive data collection.

2. Utilizing Business Intelligence Tools: Invest in business intelligence tools that can process

and analyze large datasets. Tools like Tableau, Google Analytics, or Amazon's Business Reports enable you to derive meaningful insights from complex data sets, aiding strategic decision-making.

3. Customer Segmentation: Leverage big data analytics to segment your customer base. Analyze purchasing patterns, demographics, and behaviors to identify distinct customer segments. Tailor marketing strategies, product recommendations, and communication based on these segments for more personalized and effective engagement.

4. Competitor Analysis: Use big data analytics to monitor and analyze the performance of competitors on the Amazon marketplace. Evaluate pricing strategies, product offerings, and customer reviews to gain a competitive edge and identify opportunities for differentiation.

Predictive Analytics for Inventory Management

1. Historical Sales Analysis: Analyze historical sales data to identify trends, seasonality, and demand patterns for your products. Predictive analytics can use this historical

information to forecast future sales, helping you optimize inventory levels and prevent stockouts or overstock situations.

2. Lead Time Analysis: Incorporate lead time data into predictive analytics models. By considering the time it takes for new inventory to arrive, you can optimize reorder points and maintain a more efficient inventory management system.

3. External Factors and Influences: Integrate external factors, such as holidays, promotions, or industry trends, into predictive models. This holistic approach enhances the accuracy of inventory forecasts and allows for proactive

adjustments based on anticipated changes in demand.

4.Dynamic Reorder Strategies: Implement dynamic reorder strategies that automatically adjust based on real-time data. Predictive analytics can help optimize reorder quantities and timing, ensuring that inventory aligns with changing market conditions and customer demand.

Data-DrivenMarketing Approaches

1. Customer Lifetime Value (CLV) Analysis: Calculate and analyze the Customer Lifetime Value for different customer segments. This

insight helps allocate marketing resources effectively, identifying high-value customer groups for targeted marketing campaigns.

2. Personalization through Machine Learning: Implement machine learning algorithms to personalize marketing messages based on individual customer preferences and behaviors. This data-driven approach enhances the relevance of your marketing efforts and improves customer engagement.

3. A/B Testing for Marketing Campaigns: Utilize A/B testing methodologies to assess the effectiveness of different marketing strategies. Test variables such as ad copy,

images, and promotions to understand what resonates best with your audience, optimizing future marketing campaigns.

4. Attribution Modeling: Implement advanced attribution modeling to understand the contribution of each marketing channel to conversions. Analyzing the customer journey through various touchpoints helps allocate marketing budgets more efficiently, focusing on channels that drive the most significant impact.

In conclusion, advanced analytics and data-driven decision-making in Amazon FBA involve harnessing big data for comprehensive insights, utilizing predictive analytics for efficient inventory management, and adopting data-driven marketing approaches for personalized and effective customer engagement. By embracing these advanced analytical strategies, sellers can gain a competitive advantage, optimize operations, and enhance overall business performance on the Amazon platform.

AUTOMATION TOOLS AND TECHNOLOGIES

Streamlining Operations with Automation

1.Order Processing Automation: Implement automated systems to streamline order processing. Automation tools can efficiently handle order fulfillment, reducing manual errors and improving the overall speed of order fulfillment. This includes automated order confirmation, shipping label generation, and tracking updates.

2. Inventory Management Automation: Utilize automation tools to manage inventory levels

seamlessly. Automated reorder triggers, real-time stock level monitoring, and integration with suppliers can optimize inventory management, preventing stockouts or overstock situations.

3.Customer Communication Automation: Automate customer communication processes such as order confirmations, shipping notifications, and post-purchase follow-ups. Automated emails enhance customer experience by providing timely and relevant information while reducing the workload on your end.

4. Workflow Automation: Streamline internal processes through workflow automation. Whether it's automating data entry tasks, internal communications, or approval processes, automation enhances operational efficiency, allowing your team to focus on strategic aspects of the business.

Integrating Third-Party Tools for Efficiency

1. Analytics and Reporting Tools: Integrate third-party analytics tools to complement Amazon's native analytics capabilities. Tools like Google Analytics, Sellics, or Jungle Scout

provide in-depth insights into sales performance, customer behavior, and market trends, enhancing your ability to make informed decisions.

2. Inventory Management Platforms: Explore third-party inventory management platforms to extend the capabilities of Amazon's built-in tools. Solutions like Skubana, TradeGecko, or Zoho Inventory offer advanced features for multichannel inventory synchronization, order management, and demand forecasting.

3. Marketing Automation Platforms: Integrate marketing automation platforms to streamline promotional activities. Tools like

Mailchimp, Klaviyo, or HubSpot enable automated email campaigns, customer segmentation, and personalized marketing strategies, enhancing customer engagement.

4. Shipping and Fulfillment Solutions: Consider third-party shipping and fulfillment solutions to optimize logistics. Integrating with platforms like ShipStation, Easyship, or ShipBob can simplify shipping processes, provide real-time shipping rates, and offer multiple carrier options.

Embracing AI-driven Solutions

1. Dynamic Pricing Algorithms: Implement AI-driven dynamic pricing algorithms to adjust product prices based on real-time market conditions, competitor pricing, and demand fluctuations. This dynamic approach optimizes pricing strategies for maximum competitiveness and profitability.

2. Customer Service Chatbots: Integrate AI-powered chatbots into customer service processes to handle routine inquiries, provide order status updates, and offer product recommendations. Chatbots enhance

customer support efficiency while providing instant responses to common queries.

3. Predictive Analytics for Demand Forecasting: Leverage AI-driven predictive analytics models to forecast future demand and optimize inventory levels. These models analyze historical data, market trends, and external factors to provide more accurate predictions, reducing the risk of stockouts or overstocking.

4.Image Recognition for Product Categorization: Use AI-powered image recognition technology to automate product categorization. This streamlines the listing process by automatically assigning accurate categories and attributes to products, improving discoverability and search relevance.

In summary, automation tools and technologies in Amazon FBA encompass streamlining operations through automation, integrating third-party tools for efficiency, and embracing AI-driven solutions to enhance decision-making and overall business performance. By adopting these advanced technologies, sellers can achieve higher operational efficiency, improve customer experiences, and stay competitive in the dynamic e-commerce landscape.

Leveraging Social Media for FBA Success

1. Building a Social Media Presence: Establish a strong presence on major social media platforms relevant to your target audience. Platforms like Instagram, Facebook, and Twitter can be powerful tools for engaging with potential customers and building brand awareness.

2. Content Strategy: Develop a content strategy that aligns with your brand and

resonates with your audience. Share a mix of product-focused content, behind-the-scenes glimpses, user-generated content, and educational materials. Consistent, high-quality content fosters a sense of community and enhances brand loyalty.

3. Promotional Campaigns: Use social media to run targeted promotional campaigns. This could include exclusive discounts, limited-time offers, or contests to encourage user participation. Social media promotions can drive traffic to your Amazon listings, boost sales, and create buzz around your brand.

4. Customer Engagement: Actively engage with your social media audience. Respond to comments, answer questions, and participate in discussions. By fostering two-way communication, you not only strengthen your brand's relationship with customers but also gain valuable insights into their preferences and concerns.

Influencer Marketing on Social Platforms

1. Identifying Relevant Influencers: Identify influencers in your niche or industry whose followers align with your target audience.

Look for influencers with a genuine connection to their audience and a track record of authentic engagement.

2. Building Relationships: Establish relationships with influencers through direct communication, collaborations, or by sending them samples of your products. Authentic relationships contribute to more genuine endorsements and increase the likelihood of influencers sharing your products with their followers.

3. Sponsored Content: Collaborate with influencers on sponsored content that showcases your products. Influencers can

create engaging content, such as unboxing videos, reviews, or tutorials, that highlights the benefits and features of your products. Sponsored content on social media can significantly expand your reach.

4. Measuring Impact: Utilize tracking tools to measure the impact of influencer marketing campaigns. Monitor metrics such as engagement rates, website traffic, and sales attributed to influencer collaborations. This data helps assess the effectiveness of your influencer marketing strategy.

Cross-Promotion Strategies

1. Collaborative Giveaways: Partner with other brands or influencers for collaborative giveaways. This cross-promotion strategy exposes your products to new audiences and encourages participants to follow, engage, and explore your brand further.

2. Joint Product Bundles: Explore partnerships with complementary brands to create joint product bundles. Cross-promote these bundles on social media platforms, encouraging customers to purchase related products from both brands. This strategy can

lead to increased sales and mutual brand exposure.

3. Co-Hosted Events or Webinars: Collaborate on co-hosted events, webinars, or live streams with other businesses in your industry. This not only expands your reach to their audience but also provides valuable content that can attract new followers and potential customers.

4. Affiliate Marketing Collaborations: Establish affiliate marketing collaborations with businesses that share a similar target audience. Cross-promote each other's products through affiliate links, enabling both

parties to earn a commission on sales generated from the partnership.

In conclusion, social media integration in Amazon FBA involves leveraging platforms for brand success, incorporating influencer marketing strategies for broader reach, and implementing cross-promotion strategies to collaborate with other brands. By effectively utilizing social media, sellers can create a comprehensive marketing ecosystem that enhances brand visibility, fosters customer engagement, and drives overall business growth.

BUILDING PARTNERSHIPS AND COLLABORATIONS

Forging Alliances within the Amazon Ecosystem

1. Seller Collaboration: Collaborate with other Amazon sellers to create mutually beneficial partnerships. This can include joint promotions, sharing insights on market trends, or even exploring opportunities for co-selling related products. A collaborative approach within the Amazon seller community can lead to increased visibility and shared resources.

2. Amazon FBA Networking: Engage in Amazon FBA networking events, forums, or industry conferences to connect with fellow sellers, suppliers, and service providers. Building relationships within the Amazon ecosystem can open doors to potential partnerships, knowledge exchange, and shared strategies for success.

3. Leveraging Amazon Services: Explore partnerships with other businesses that offer complementary services within the Amazon ecosystem. This could involve teaming up with Amazon consultants, photographers, or

logistics providers to enhance the overall efficiency of your FBA operations.

4. Collaborative Product Launches: Consider collaborating with other sellers to launch complementary products simultaneously. Coordinated product launches can create a buzz, attract a wider audience, and leverage cross-promotional opportunities within the Amazon marketplace.

Collaborative Marketing Initiatives

1. Co-Marketing Campaigns: Partner with other brands or sellers on co-marketing campaigns. This can include joint advertising

efforts, sharing social media channels, or co-sponsoring events. Co-marketing amplifies your reach by tapping into each other's audiences and resources.

2. Content Collaboration: Collaborate on content creation, such as blog posts, videos, or webinars, with businesses that share a similar target audience. This collaborative content can be shared across both parties' platforms, expanding your brand's exposure and providing valuable information to your audience.

3. Affiliate Marketing Partnerships: Explore affiliate marketing partnerships with

businesses that align with your niche. By leveraging affiliate relationships, you can earn commissions on sales generated through mutual promotions. This incentivizes both parties to actively promote each other's products.

4. Social Media Takeovers: Engage in social media takeovers with other brands or influencers. Allow them to take control of your social media for a day or week, showcasing their perspective, products, or behind-the-scenes content. This cross-promotion strategy introduces your brand to a new audience.

Exploring Joint Ventures in E-commerce

1. Identifying Complementary Businesses: Identify businesses in the e-commerce space that offer complementary products or services. Joint ventures can be formed with companies that enhance your overall offering or cater to a similar customer base.

2. Shared Resources and Expertise: Partner with businesses that bring unique resources or expertise to the table. This could involve collaborating with a tech-savvy partner for website development, a logistics expert for

efficient shipping, or a marketing agency for strategic promotional campaigns.

3.Risk and Investment Sharing: Joint ventures enable the sharing of risks and investments in new ventures or projects. Whether it's expanding to new markets, developing innovative products, or launching a shared e-commerce platform, partnerships can provide additional resources and mitigate individual business risks.

4. Legal Agreements and Clear Terms: When exploring joint ventures, ensure that legal agreements clearly outline the terms, responsibilities, and expectations of each

party. This includes profit-sharing arrangements, decision-making processes, and exit strategies in case the partnership evolves or concludes.

In summary, building partnerships and collaborations in Amazon FBA involves forging alliances within the Amazon ecosystem, engaging in collaborative marketing initiatives, and exploring joint ventures in the broader e-commerce landscape. These partnerships can lead to increased visibility, shared resources, and strategic advantages that contribute to the

growth and success of your FBA business.

CONTINUOUS LEARNING AND ADAPTATION

Staying Updated on E-commerce Trends

1. Industry Publications and Blogs: Regularly read e-commerce industry publications, blogs, and news sources to stay informed about the latest trends, market shifts, and emerging technologies. This continuous learning ensures you're well-equipped to adapt your Amazon FBA business to evolving industry dynamics.

2. Podcasts and Webinars: Listen to podcasts and attend webinars focused on e-commerce and Amazon FBA. These platforms often feature industry experts, successful sellers, and thought leaders who share valuable insights, strategies, and real-world experiences that can inform your decision-making.

3. Subscription to Newsletters: Subscribe to newsletters from reputable e-commerce platforms, marketplaces, and industry influencers. Newsletters often provide curated updates, analysis, and exclusive content that can enhance your understanding

of market trends and inform your business strategies.

4. E-learning Platforms: Explore e-learning platforms that offer courses and certifications in e-commerce, digital marketing, and Amazon FBA. Platforms like Udemy, Coursera, or specialized e-commerce training programs provide structured learning experiences to deepen your expertise.

Participating in Amazon Seller Forums and Communities

1. Active Participation: Join Amazon seller forums and online communities to actively

participate in discussions, share experiences, and seek advice from fellow sellers. Platforms like Seller Central Forums, Reddit's Amazon Seller community, or specialized Facebook groups provide valuable insights and a sense of community.

2. Ask Questions and Seek Guidance: Don't hesitate to ask questions and seek guidance from experienced sellers. Seller forums are excellent resources for troubleshooting issues, gaining perspective on challenges, and accessing collective knowledge within the Amazon seller community.

3. Networking Opportunities: Engage in networking opportunities within these communities. Connecting with other sellers, industry experts, and service providers can open doors to collaborations, partnerships, and shared learning experiences. Attend virtual or in-person events organized by these communities for additional networking opportunities.

4. Staying Informed on Policy Changes: Seller forums often serve as platforms for discussions around policy changes and updates from Amazon. Staying informed about these changes is crucial for adapting

your business practices to remain compliant and optimize your seller performance.

Professional Development Opportunities

1. Amazon Seller Workshops: Participate in Amazon Seller workshops and training sessions. Amazon frequently conducts webinars and workshops to educate sellers on new features, best practices, and strategies for success. These sessions provide direct insights from Amazon experts.

2. Industry Conferences and Events: Attend e-commerce and Amazon FBA conferences,

both virtual and in-person. These events offer opportunities to learn from industry leaders, connect with fellow sellers, and gain exposure to the latest tools and technologies shaping the e-commerce landscape.

3. Mentorship Programs: Seek mentorship from experienced sellers or industry professionals. Mentorship programs, whether formal or informal, provide personalized guidance, advice, and a wealth of practical knowledge that can accelerate your professional development.

4. Continuous Skill-building: Invest in continuous skill-building through online

courses, workshops, or certifications. Enhance your expertise in areas such as digital marketing, data analysis, and customer service to stay competitive and adaptable in the ever-changing e-commerce environment.

Continuous learning and adaptation in Amazon FBA involve staying updated on e-commerce trends, actively participating in seller forums and communities, and seizing professional development opportunities. By embracing a mindset of continuous improvement and staying connected with industry developments, sellers can navigate challenges, capitalize on opportunities, and foster long-term success in the dynamic world of Amazon FBA.

CONCLUSION

Recap of Key Points

In this comprehensive exploration of Amazon FBA, I've covered essential aspects of establishing and optimizing an e-commerce business on the world's largest online marketplace. From the foundational steps of setting up your account to advanced strategies like international selling and leveraging emerging technologies, the journey through Amazon FBA is dynamic and multifaceted.

Key points highlighted include: **the importance of strategic product selection, compliance with Amazon's policies, and the seamless fulfillment process facilitated by Amazon's extensive network of fulfillment centers.** I delved into challenges that sellers may encounter and provided solutions, emphasizing the need for proactive inventory management, customer-centric approaches, and continuous adaptation to market changes.

Final Tips for Amazon FBA Success

1. Continuous Learning: The e-commerce landscape is ever-evolving. Stay informed about industry trends, changes in Amazon policies, and emerging technologies. Engage in continuous learning to adapt your strategies and stay ahead of the competition.

2. Customer Satisfaction: Prioritize customer satisfaction as a cornerstone of your business. Responsive customer service, genuine engagement with customer feedback, and a commitment to delivering quality products contribute significantly to long-term success.

3.Strategic Expansion: Explore opportunities for expanding your product lines, reaching new markets, and diversifying your business. Embrace advanced strategies like private labeling, seasonal offerings, and international selling to fuel growth.

4. Data-Driven Decision-Making: Leverage analytics tools and data-driven insights to make informed business decisions. Regularly monitor key performance metrics, analyze customer behavior, and adjust your strategies based on actionable data.

Encqouragement for Future Growth

As you navigate the dynamic landscape of Amazon FBA, remember that success is a journey, not a destination. Embrace challenges as opportunities to learn and grow. The e-commerce industry is filled with possibilities, and your dedication to innovation and customer satisfaction positions you for a future of sustained growth. Continue to adapt, experiment with new approaches, and remain resilient in the face of challenges. The skills and insights gained from your Amazon FBA journey are invaluable assets that will contribute to your success not only on the platform but also in the broader realm of e-commerce.

In the spirit of continuous improvement and entrepreneurial spirit, I encourage you to envision the limitless potential of your Amazon FBA business. With dedication, strategic thinking, and a commitment to excellence, your journey in the world of e-commerce holds the promise of enduring success and fulfillment.

Best of luck on your continued Amazon

FBA adventure!

www.ingramcontent.com/pod-product-compliance
Lightning Source LLC
Chambersburg PA
CBHW071204290526
45796CB00008B/139